I0157998

California - A State in Verse

California in the 20th Century became an almost mythical place of stunning scenery, glamorous industries, and fabled places; Hollywood, LA, San Francisco, as well as a people and culture that varied from wacko to incredibly creative. It was where the world wanted to be and took its lead from.

From an earlier history as home to many Native American tribes it was taken by Spain to become part of its huge Americas Empire. After a successful war of independence from Spain, Mexico became a vast, but weak, sovereign nation. After a war with the United States this huge area from Texas to California was settled into the States we know today.

As citizens made their way west, initially with the California Gold Rush, also in 1848, in search of better lives poets travelled too and over the decades documented their feelings about their land – California. Others, including Robert Louis Stevenson and Mark Twain may only have been passing through but what they found their demanded written confirmation. In this collection of California Versed poets share something that is uniquely Californian.

Index of Poems

A Bird Sings in My Heart by Irene Hardy
I Know Not How It Is with You by Robert Louis Stevenson
Politics by Ambrose Bierce
El Vaquero by Lucius Harwood Foote
California Skies by Clarence Urmy
Yosemite by Daniel S. Richardson
Junipero Serra by Richard Edward White
To the Colorado Desert by Madge Morris Wagner
Music by Edward Robeson Taylor
Mankind (excerpt) by Joaquin Miller
Indirection by Richard Realf
Christmas in California (excerpt) by Edward Rowland Sill
Luke by F. Bret Harte
The Comet by Charles Warren Stoddard
Belle of Monterey by Einnim Havemeyer Tucker
"The Pride of Battery B" by Frank H. Gassaway
The Celestial Surgeon by Robert Louis Stevenson
A Californian's Dreams Poem by Edward Rowland Sill

Present Period, 1890 to 1915
Invocation to California by Charles Keeler
The Black Vulture by George Sterling
Resurgam by David Lesser Lezinsky
Just California by John S. McGroarty
The Happiest Heart by John Vance Cheney
The Creed of Desire by Bruce Porter
To San Francisco by Samuel John Alexander
The Shrine of Song by Louis Alexander Robertson
The Rosary by Robert Cameron Rogers
Lines by Yone Noguchi
The Old Brooch by Charles F. Lummis
The Wolves of the Sea by Herbert Bashford
A Dream of Beauty by Clark Ashton Smith
Women's Eyes by Arthur William Ryder
The Goblin Laugh by Edwin Markham
The Awakening by Christian Binkley
A Nosegay by Augustin S. Macdonald
Appearances by William Henry Hudson
The Grave of Pompey by Sister Anthony, S.N.D.
Vivérols by David Starr Jordan
A Memory by Carolus Ager (Charles Kellogg Field)
A Toast by Gelett Burgess
To the Average Man by Wallace Irwin
Twilight Town by Ralph Erwin Gibbs
Growth of the Soul by James Henry MacLafferty
To My Ink-Well by Lionel Josaphare
To a Star-Flower by Edward Howard Griggs
Little Memories by Nora May French
The Difference by Augustin S. Macdonald
Lyric by Howard V. Sutherland
Nirvana by Bernard Westermann

California by Bayard Taylor

O fair young land, the youngest, fairest far
Of which our world can boast—
Whose guardian planet, evening's silver star,
Illumes thy golden coast,

How art thou conquered, tamed in all the pride
Of savage beauty still!
How brought, O panther of the splendid hide,
To know thy master's will!

No more thou sittest on thy tawny hills
In indolent repose;
Or pourest the crystal of a thousand rills

Down from thy house of snows.

But where the wild oats wrapped thy knees in gold,
The plowman drives his share,
And where, through cañons deep, thy streams are rolled,
The miner's arm is bare.

Yet in thy lap, thus rudely rent and torn,
A nobler seed shall be;
Mother of mighty men, thou shalt not mourn
Thy lost virginity!

Thy human children shall restore the grace
Gone with thy fallen pines;
The wild, barbaric beauty of thy face
Shall round to classic lines.

And order, justice, social law shall curb
Thy untamed energies;
And art and science, with their dreams superb,
Replace thine ancient ease.

The marble, sleeping in thy mountains now,
Shall live in sculptures rare;
Thy native oak shall crown the sage's brow—
Thy bay, the poet's hair.

Thy tawny hills shall bleed their purple wine,
Thy valleys yield their oil;
And music, with her eloquence divine,
Persuade thy sons to toil.

Till Hesper, as he trims his silver beam,
No happier land shall see,
And earth shall find her old Arcadian dream
Restored again in thee!

The Golden Gate by "Caxton"—(W. H. Rhodes)

Old Thebes could boast of her gates of brass,
As they grated on hinges hoary,
And loosened their bolts for a monarch to pass,
On his errands of guilt and glory.

But their portals were closed on a nation of slaves,
Kneeling low at the foot of a Pharaoh,
And the Nile now waters an Egypt of graves,
From sepulchral Philæ, to Cairo.

Remorseless Time, in his journeying's on,
Like Samson, at Gaza, of old,
On his shoulders her hundred gates have bore,
And covered their sheen with mold.

But further than Ind, in the western world,
Unknown to the sages olden,
Young Freedom, at length, has her banner unfurled,
In a city whose Gate is Golden.

Its glittering bars are the breakers high,
Its hinges are hills of granite,
Its bolts are the winds, its arch is the sky,
Its corner-stone a planet!

Inside of its portals no slave bows his head,
To priestess of On or of Isis,
Or covers the ground a monarch may tread,
With the slime of a minion's kisses.

But proud of his home in a city so fair,
Enthroned on her hillocks seven,
He stands like a Roman, and breathes the free air,
And kneels to no God, but in heaven.

No giant can tear from their pillars away,
The Golden Gate of his glory,
For as long as the winds and the waters play,
It shall swing on its hinges hoary.

The Song of the Flume by Anna M. Fitch

Awake, awake! for my track is red,
With the glow of the coming day;
And with tinkling tread, from my dusty bed,
I haste o'er the hills away,
Up from the valley, up from the plain,
Up from the river's side;
For I come with a gush, and a torrent's rush,
And there's wealth in my swelling tide.

I am fed by the melting rills that start
Where the sparkling snow-peaks gleam,
My voice is free, and with fiercest glee
I leap in the sun's broad beam;
Tho' torn from the channels deep and old,
I have worn through the craggy hill,
Yet I flow in pride, as my waters glide,
And there's mirth in my music still.

I sought the shore of the sounding sea,
From the far Sierra's hight,
With a starry breast, and a snow-capped crest
I foamed in a path of light;
But they bore me thence in a winding way,
The've fettered me like a slave,
And as scarfs of old were exchanged for gold,
So they barter my soil-stained wave.

Thro' the deep tunnel, down the dark shaft,
I search for the shining ore;
Hoist it away to the light of day,
Which it never has seen before.
Spade and shovel, mattock and pick,
Ply them with eager haste;
For my golden shower is sold by the hour,
And the drops are too dear to waste.

Lift me aloft to the mountain's brow,
Fathom the deep "blue vein,"
And I'll sift the soil for the shining spoil,
As I sink to the valley again.
The swell of my swarthy breast shall bear
Pebble and rock away,
Though they brave my strength, they shall yield at length,
But the glittering gold shall stay.

Mine is no stern and warrior march,
No stormy trump and drum;
No banners gleam in my darkened stream,
As with conquering step I come;
But I touch the tributary earth
Till it owns a monarch's sway,
And with eager hand, from a conquered land,
I bear its wealth away.

Awake, awake! there are living hearts
In the lands you've left afar;
There are tearful eyes in the homes you prize
As they gaze on the western star;
Then up from the valley, up from the hill,
Up from the river's side;
For I come with a gush, and a torrent's rush,
And there's wrath in my swelling tide.

The Sabbath Bells by John R. Ridge

The Sabbath bells are ringing

With clear and cheerful notes,
And from the steeple springing,
Far off the music floats.

To yonder mountain reaches,
The ever rising strain,
And Echo's dying speeches
Repeat it o'er again.

The summer woodlands filling,
The solemn cadence rolls,
And through the leaves is thrilling
Like soft, pulsating souls.

The air with rippling motion,
Aeolian answer gives,
And like a trembling ocean,
Its outspread bosom heaves.

The far horizon sweeping,
Each tone majestic swells,
And all the world is leaping
Beneath the sounding bells.

'Tis solemn, yet 'tis cheerful,
A clear and pleasant voice.
That bids the sad and tearful
Be hopeful and rejoice.

Let Sabbath morns unclouded
Still hear these tones of peace.
For earth with woe is shrouded
When Sabbath bells shall cease.

An Evening Song at Sea by C. E. Havens

Sweet night, whence sweeter calm doth flow,
Sweet solitude of sea and sky:
Made sweeter far, because I know
That thou with all sweet things must die;
For beauty fades from out the eye,
And love itself will cease to be;
As summer winds from tropic shores,
Die on the smooth unruffled sea.

Now, Hesperus, evening star of love
Flings o'er the waves a lane of light;
And constellations from above
Gleam out like di'mond on the sight:

And phosphor, glinting silver-white
From out the deep and dimpled sea,
Looks like another realm of stars
In Heaven's inverted canopy.

Sweet double star of love and rest,
That usherest in the hour of sleep;
I watch in grief thy waning crest
Go glimmering down the dusky deep.
While other stars their vespers keep,
My longing thoughts revert to thee,
And follow up thy trail of light
To other heavens beyond the sea.

To the Sierras by J. J. Owen

Ye snow-capped mountains, basking in the sun,
Like fleecy clouds that deck the summer skies,
On you I gaze, when day's dull task is done,
Till night shuts out your glories from my eyes.

For stormy turmoil, and ambition's strife,
I find in you a solace and a balm,—
Derive a higher purpose, truer life,
From your pale splendor, passionless and calm.

Mellowed by distance, all your rugged cliffs,
And deep ravines, in graceful outlines lie;
Each giant form in silent grandeur lifts
Its hoary summit to the evening sky.

I reck not of the wealth untold, concealed
Beneath your glorious coronal of snows,
Whose budding treasure yet but scarce revealed,
Should blossom into trade—a golden rose.

A mighty realm is waking at your feet
To life and beauty, from the lap of Time,
With cities vast, where millions yet shall meet,
And Peace shall reign in majesty sublime.

Rock-ribbed Sierras, with your crests of snow,
A type of manhood, ever strong and true,
Whose heart with golden wealth should ever glow,
Whose thoughts in purity should symbol you.

To My Mother by Stephen C. Massett

My Mother! canst thou see me now
From the far-off fields of light—
Canst thou in spirit come again,
And bless me with thy sight?
Oh! I can see thee, when these eyes
Are closed in balmy sleep;
And reveling in happy dreams
We sweet communion keep!

Years, years have passed, and life to me
Has been but as a dream,
Yet often have I yearned for thee,
As sailing down its stream,
Fond memory brings thee back again,
As thou wert once to me:
When nestled in thy arms I lay,
Or crept upon thy knee!

And when I saw thee in that sleep
From which there is no waking,
And felt as I then gazed on thee
My very heart was breaking;
Oh! can it be, that in that land,
Where there is no more pain,
We may once more united be,
Never to part again?

And shall we meet as we have met,
And be as we have been—
And shall I see thee on me smile,
As I have sometimes seen?
Oh God! if this it is to meet
In Heaven's own land of light,
Illume my path—direct my feet,
And guide my steps aright!

The Lone Pine by B. P. Avery

Sway thy top, thou ancient pine—
Warrior of the storm commanding!
Lone upon the mountain standing,
Whom no ivy's arms entwine.
Melancholy souls like mine,
'Neath thy shadow passing slow,
Love to hear thy plaintive moan;
'Tis an echo of the woe
Found in human breasts alone.

Mournfully amid the ruins
Of thy fellows standest thou,
Like a column of some temple
Living but in story now;
All around it, wildly scattered,
Fallen walls and pillars shattered.
Softly sighing through thy branches
Sounds the wind, with fall and swell;
Now retreats, and now advances,
Rousing fancy with its spell,
Like the melody that chances
On the ear from distant bell,
Or the murmur that entrances
Of the tinted sea-side shell.
Lo! musing on thy loneliness,
Thy brethren seem again to rise;
On every hand a wilderness
Shuts out the prospect of the skies.

'Tis verdure all, and deepest shade, no sound
Disturbs the thoughtful silence, save
A murmur such as rolls through Ocean cave,
And rustling of dry leaves upon the ground.
But while I listen with an awe profound,
A glance dispels the visionary wood—
A single tree remains where late ten thousand stood.

No Baby in the House by Clara Dolliver

No baby in the house I know—
'Tis far too nice and clean;
No toys by careless fingers strewn
Upon the floors are seen.
No finger-marks are on the panes,
No scratches on the chairs,
No wooden men set up in rows,
Or marshaled off in pairs;
No little stockings to be darned,
All ragged at the toes,
No pile of mending to be done,
Made up of baby-clothes;
No little troubles to be soothed,
No little hands to fold;
No grimy fingers to be washed,
No stories to be told;
No tender kisses to be given,
No nick-names—"Clove" and "Mouse;"
No merry frolics after tea—
No baby in the house.

The Parting Hour (excerpt) by Edward Pollock

There's something in the "parting hour,"
Will chill the warmest heart,
Yet kindred, comrades, lovers, friends,
Are fated all to part;
But this I've seen—and many a pang
Has pressed it on my mind—
The one that goes is happier
Than those he leaves behind.

Truth by G.

Truth, like the diamond, is a fount of light,
Beaming effulgent in the darkest night;
Error its ebon form may intervene,
But still it beams as brightly, though unseen;
And though thus hid till centuries have past,
The steady fire shall slay the foe at last.
Dark clouds may sometimes veil its radiant form,
And lightning rend it;—but, amid the storm,
The gem is undefiled, and its pure ray
Brighter shall shine, like sunbeams on the day
When storm, and cloud, and lightning pass away.

The Whole Story by J. F. Bowman

When Jones was sixteen, he was bent
On one day being President.

At twenty-five, Jones thought that he
Content as District Judge would be.

At thirty, he was much elated
When Mayor of Frogtown nominated.

But bootless all the nomination—
His rival Tompkins graced the station.

At forty-five, his dreams had fled;
Hope and Ambition, both were dead.

When from his toils he found release,
He died—a Justice of the Peace.

O youthful heart, so high and bold,
Thus is thy brief, sad story told!

To My First Love by Crowquill

This heart has beat to many a one,
To many, passing fair;
But oh! the Love which first it knew,
Still lingers fondly there;
Though brighter eyes have beamed on me,
And rosier lips I've prest,
The Love which first I felt for thee—
Yet dwells within my breast.

Tho' softer skies are o'er me now,
And stars shine brighter here;
Tho' Nature wears a sunny smile
And birds sing all the year,
Yet I would fain them all resign,
To dwell once more with thee,
For one sweet smile from lips like thine,   1
Were dearer far to me.

As memory clings around the spot,
Where first the breath we drew,
And all our kindlier thoughts are placed
On scenes that first we knew—
So earliest Love still twines around
The heart which beats to ours,
As Summer's sweetest dew is found
Upon the earliest flowers.

Song of Labor; the Miner by John Swett

The Eastern sky is blushing red,
The distant hill-top glowing;
The brook is murmuring in its bed,
In idle frolics flowing;
'Tis time the pickaxe and the spade,
And iron "tom" were ringing,
And with ourselves, the mountain stream,
A song of labor singing.

The mountain air is cool and fresh,
Unclouded skies bend o'er us,
Broad placers, rich in hidden gold,

Lie temptingly before us;
We ask no magic Midas' wand,
Nor wizard rod divining,
The pickaxe, spade and brawny hand
Are sorcerers in mining.

When labor ceases with the day,
To simple fare returning,
We gather in a merry group
Around the camp-fires burning;
The mountain sod our couch at night,
The stars shine bright above us,
We think of home and fall asleep,
To dream of those who love us.

Stanzas by Sarah E. Carmichael

I love the music of the wave,
I love the night wind's song;
I love to hear the storm king cheer
His frenzied host along;
I love all nature's thrilling tones,
I love the notes of art—
But better far, than all, I love
The music of the heart.

I love the tints of beauty laid
Softly on leaf and flower;
The trembling light that gilds the night,
And wraps the midnight hour;
I love the sunny warmth and light
From the glad sunbeams stole—
But better far, than all, I love
The beauty of the soul.

I prize all heaven's precious gifts,
Laid on the earth or sea;
The lowliest flower that decks life's bower
Is beautiful to me:
I value every ray of light
That gleams below—above;
But, oh! I value more than these
The smiles of those I love.

Hurrah for the Next that Dies! by Bartholomew Dowling

[This remarkable poem relates to revelry in India at a time when the English officers serving in that country were being struck down by pestilence. It has been correctly styled "the very poetry of military despair."]

We meet 'neath the sounding rafter,
And the walls around are bare:
As they shout back our peals of laughter,
It seems as the dead were there.
Then stand to your glasses!—steady!
We drink 'fore our comrades' eyes;
One cup to the dead already:
Hurrah for the next that dies!

Not here are the goblets glowing,
Not here is the vintage sweet;
'Tis cold as our hearts are growing,
And dark as the doom we meet.
But stand to your glasses!—steady!
And soon shall our pulses rise.
One cup to the dead already:
Hurrah for the next that dies!

There's many a hand that's shaking,
And many a cheek that's sunk;
But soon, though our hearts are breaking,
They'll burn with the wine we've drunk.
Then stand to your glasses!—steady!
'Tis here the revival lies;
Quaff a cup to the dead already:
Hurrah for the next that dies!

Time was when we laughed at others;
We thought we were wiser then.
Ha! ha! let them think of their mothers,
Who hope to see them again.
No! Stand to your glasses!—steady!
The thoughtless is here the wise;
One cup to the dead already:
Hurrah for the next that dies!

Not a sigh for the lot that darkles,
Not a tear for the friends that sink;
We'll fall 'mid the wine-cup's sparkles,
As mute as the wine we drink.
Come! Stand to your glasses!—steady!
'Tis this that the respite buys;
One cup to the dead already:
Hurrah for the next that dies!

Who dreads to the dust returning?
Who shrinks from the sable shore,

Where the high and haughty yearning
Of the soul can sting no more?
No! Stand to your glasses!—steady!
This world is a world of lies;
One cup to the dead already:
Hurrah for the next that dies!

Cut off from the land that bore us,
Betray'd by the land we find,
When the brightest are gone before us,
And the dullest are left behind.
Stand!—stand to your glasses!—steady!
'Tis all we have left to prize;
One cup to the dead already:
Hurrah for the next that dies!

Scotland by James Linen

My country! My country! I'll love thee forever!
Pair land of my birth; I forget thee will never:
Though severed from thee by the deep-heaving main,
Hope's whispers still tell me I'll see thee again—
Truth reigning triumphant, by shores uninvaded,
Thy beauty unshorn, and thy Thistle unfaded.

When Summer makes Nature her glories disclose,
When Winter is robed in her mantle of snows,
And withers the flowerets that deck the gay scene,
Thy Thistle stands forth in its garment of green.
Proud emblem of freedom! disdaining to crouch,
The tyrant reels back at its deep-piercing touch;

He cannot, he dare not, its beauty deform,
For boldly it stands 'mid the tempest and storm.
Oh! long may it wave on the green mountain side,
Unfading as Truth in the strength of its pride:
Then spare it, O Time, from the wrecks of decay,
Till Nature expires and the hills melt away.

Columbus by Joaquin Miller

Behind him lay the gray Azores,
Behind the Gates of Hercules;
Before him on the ghost of shores,
Before him only shoreless seas.
The good mate said: "Now we must pray,
For lo, the very stars are gone.

Brave Adm'r'l speak; what shall I say?"
"Why say: 'Sail on! sail on! sail on!'"

"My men grow mutinous day by day;
My men grow ghastly wan and weak."
The stout mate thought of home; a spray
Of salt wave washed his swarthy cheek.
"What shall I say, brave Adm'r'l, say,
If we sight naught but seas at dawn!"
"Why you shall say at break of day:
'Sail on! sail on! sail on! sail on!'"

They sailed and sailed, as the winds might blow
Until at last the blanched mate said:
"Why, not even God would know
Should I and all my men fall dead.
These very winds forgot their way,
For God from these dread seas is gone,
Now speak, brave Adm'r'l; speak and say"—
He said: "Sail on! sail on! sail on!"

They sailed. They sailed. Then spake the mate:
"This mad sea shows its teeth tonight.
He curls his lips, he lies in wait,
With lifted teeth, as if to bite!
Brave Adm'r'l, say but one good word;
What shall we do when hope is gone!"
The words leapt as a leaping sword:
"Sail on! sail on! sail on! sail on!"

Then, pale and worn, he kept his deck,
And peered through darkness. Ah, that night
Of all dark nights! And then a speck—
A light! A light! A light! A light!
It grew, a starlit flag unfurled!
It grew to be Time's burst of dawn.
He gained a world; he gave that world
Its grandest lesson: "On! sail on!"

To Mrs. M— by Richard Realf

On the birth of her first child

When you lay shivering with the great excess
Of mother-marvel at your child's first cry;
When you looked up and saw him standing by,
Leaning the strong unspeakable utterness
Of all his soul upon you; when you smiled,
And your weak lips strove mightily to frame

To a new song your new life's oriflamme,
And presently the infinite words, "Our child,"
Made a most musical murmur, as of breath
Breathed by a poet's spirit—did you know
The babe's slight moan, that seemed so faint and low,
Was God's voice speaking from dear Nazareth,
Covering you up with that white light that lay
On Mary and her young Christ in the hay?

Among The Redwoods by Edward Rowland Sill

Farewell to such a world! Too long I press
The crowded pavement with unwilling feet.
Pity makes pride, and hate breeds hatefulness.
And both are poisons. In the forest, sweet
The shade, the peace! Immensity, that seems
To drown the human life of doubts and dreams.

Far off the massive portals of the wood,
Buttressed with shadow, misty-blue, serene,
Waited my coming. Speedily I stood
Where the dun wall rose roofed in plumy green.
Dare one go in? — Glance backward! Dusk as night
Each column, fringed with sprays of amber light.

Let me, along this fallen bole, at rest,
Turn to the cool, dim roof my glowing face.
Delicious dark on weary eyelids prest!
Enormous solitude of silent space,
But for a low and thunderous ocean sound,
Too far to hear, felt thrilling through the ground!

No stir nor call the sacred hush profanes;
Save when from some bare treetop, far on high,
Fierce disputations of the clamorous cranes
Fall muffled, as from out the upper sky.
So still, one dreads to wake the dreaming air,
Breaks a twig softly, moves the foot with care.

The hollow dome is green with empty shade,
Struck through with slanted shafts of afternoon;
Aloft, a little rift of blue is made,
Where slips a ghost that last night was the moon;
Beside its pearl a sea-cloud stays its wing,
Beneath a tilted hawk is balancing.

The heart feels not in every time and mood
What is around it. Dull as any stone
I lay; then, like a darkening dream, the wood

Grew Karnak's temple, where I breathed alone
In the awed air strange incense, and uprose
Dim, monstrous columns in their dread repose.

The mind not always sees; but if there shine
A bit of fern-lace bending over moss,
A silky glint that rides a spider-line,
On a trefoil two shadow-spears that cross,
Three grasses that toss up their nodding heads,
With spring and curve like clustered fountain-threads,

Suddenly, through side windows of the eye,
Deep solitudes, where never souls have met;
Vast spaces, forest corridors that lie
In a mysterious world, unpeopled yet.
Because the outward eye elsewhere was caught,
The awfulness and wonder come unsought.

If death be but resolving back again
Into the world's deep soul, this is a kind
Of quiet, happy death, untouched by pain
Or sharp reluctance. For I feel my mind
Is interfused with all I hear and see;
As much a part of All as cloud or tree.

Listen! A deep and solemn wind on high;
The shafts of shining dust shift to and fro;
The columned trees sway imperceptibly,
And creak as mighty masts when trade-winds blow.
The cloudy sails are set; the earth-ship swings
Along the sea of space to grander things.

The Angelus by F. Bret Harte

Heard at the Mission Dolores, 1868

Bells of the Past, whose long-forgotten music
Still fills the wide expanse,
Tingeing the sober twilight of the Present
With color of romance:

I hear your call, and see the sun descending
On rock and wave and sand,
As down the coast the Mission voices blending
Girdle the heathen land.

Within the circle of your incantation
No blight nor mildew falls;
Nor fierce unrest, nor lust, nor low ambition

Passes those airy walls.

Borne on the swell of your long waves receding,
I touch the farther Past,—
I see the dying glow of Spanish glory,
The sunset dream and last!

Before me rise the dome-shaped Mission towers,
The white Presidio;
The swart commander in his leathern jerkin,
The priest in stole of snow.

Once more I see Portola's cross uplifting
Above the setting sun;
And past the headland, northward, slowly drifting
The freighted galleon.

O solemn bells! whose consecrated masses
Recall the faith of old,—
O tinkling bells! that lulled with twilight music
The spiritual fold!

Your voices break and falter in the darkness,—
Break, falter, and are still;
And veiled and mystic, like the Host descending,
The sun sinks from the hill!

Madrigal by Charles Warren Stoddard

A maid is seated by a brook,
The sweetest of sweet creatures;
I pass that way with my good book,
But cannot read, nor cease to look
Upon her winsome features.

Amongst the blushes on her cheek
Her small white hand reposes,
I am a shepherd, for I seek
That willful lamb, with fleece so sleek,
Feeding among the roses.

Lines by Mark Twain

On His Wife's Tombstone

Warm summer sun,
Shine kindly here.

Warm southern wind,
Blow softly here.
Green sod above,
Lie light, lie light.
Good night, dear heart,
Good night, good night.

Home by Edward Rowland Sill

There lies a little city in the hills;
White are its roofs, dim is each dwelling's door,
And peace with perfect rest its bosom fills.

There the pure mist, the pity of the sea,
Comes as a white, soft hand, and reaches o'er
And touches its still face most tenderly.

Unstirred and calm, amid our shifting years,
Lo! where it lies, far from the clash and roar,
With quiet distance blurred, as if thro' tears.

O heart, that prayest so for God to send
Some loving messenger to go before
And lead the way to where thy longings end,

Be sure, be very sure, that soon will come
His kindest angel, and through that still door
Into the Infinite love will lead thee home.

In Blossom Time by Ina Coolbrith

It's o my heart, my heart,
To be out in the sun and sing—
To sing and shout in the fields about,
In the balm and the blossoming!

Sing loud, O bird in the tree;
O bird, sing loud in the sky,
And honey-bees, blacken the clover beds—
There is none of you glad as I.

The leaves laugh low in the wind,
Laugh low, with the wind at play;
And the odorous call of the flowers all
Entices my soul away!

For O but the world is fair, is fair—

And O but the world is sweet!
I will out in the gold of the blossoming mould,
And sit at the Master's feet.

And the love my heart would speak,
I will fold in the lily's rim,
That th' lips of the blossom, more pure and meek,
May offer it up to Him.

Then sing in the hedgerow green, O thrush,
O skylark, sing in the blue;
Sing loud, sing clear, that the King may hear,
And my soul shall sing with you!

Sweethearts and Wives by Daniel O'Connell

If sweethearts were sweethearts always,
Whether as maid or wife,
No drop would be half so pleasant
In the mingled draught of life.

But the sweetheart has smiles and blushes
When the wife has frowns and sighs,
And the wife's have a wrathful glitter
For the glow of the sweetheart's eyes.

If lovers were lovers always,
The same to sweetheart and wife,
Who would change for a future of Eden
The joys of this checkered life?

But husbands grow grave and silent,
And cares on the anxious brow
Oft replace the sunshine that perished
At the words of the marriage vow.

Happy is he whose sweetheart
Is wife and sweetheart still—
Whose voice, as of old, can charm;
Whose kiss, as of old, can thrill;

Who has plucked the rose, to find ever
Its beauty and fragrance increase,
As the flush of passion is mellowed
In love's unmeasured peace;

Who sees in the step a lightness;
Who finds in the form a grace;
Who reads an unaltered brightness

In the witchery of the face,

Undimmed and unchanged. Ah! happy
Is he crowned with such a life,
Who drinks the wife, pledging the sweetheart,
And toasts in the sweetheart the wife.

Two Truths by Helen Hunt Jackson

"Darling," he said, "I never meant
To hurt you;" and his eyes grew wet.
"I would not hurt you for the world!
Am I to blame if I forget?"

"Forgive my selfish tears!" she cried.
"Forgive! I knew that it was not
That you would mean to hurt me, love;
I knew it was that you forgot!"

But, all the same, deep in her heart
Rankled this thought, and rankles yet:
When love is at its best, one loves
So much that he cannot forget!

A Bird Sings in My Heart by Irene Hardy

A bird sings in the garden of my heart,
And all day long I hear its carol clear;
At night it folds its gentle wings so near,
Its tender pulsings stir my blood and start
The tears within my eyes to think Love's art
Should stay her wings with me and make so dear
The rude wild bowers of my demesne, nor fear
But she should find her spirit's counterpart.
All day I go resolved and thinking how
To make more sweet for her that garden place;
How I will pluck away the weeds, the rose
Of Love to plant there for her nesting-bough;
How I will school my heart to every grace
That it may be her home, her one repose.

I Know Not How It Is with You by Robert Louis Stevenson

I know not how it is with you—
I love the first and last,

The whole field of the present view,
The whole flow of the past.

One tittle of the things that are,
Nor you should change nor I—
One pebble in our path—one star
In all our heaven of sky.

Our lives, and every day and hour,
One sympathy appear:
One road, one garden—every flower
And every bramble dear.

Politics by Ambrose Bierce

That land full surely hastens to its end
Where public sycophants in homage bend
The populace to flatter, and repeat
The doubled echoes of its loud conceit.
Lowly their attitude but high their aim,
They creep to eminence through paths of shame,
Till fixed securely in the seats of pow'r,
The dupes they flattered they at last devour.

El Vaquero by Lucius Harwood Foote

Tinged with the blood of Aztec lands,
Sphinx-like, the tawny herdsman stands,
A coiled reata in his hands.
Devoid of hope, devoid of fear,
Half brigand, and half cavalier,
This helot, with imperial grace,
Wears ever on his tawny face
A sad, defiant look of pain.
Left by the fierce iconoclast
A living fragment of the past,—
Greek of the Greeks he must remain.

California Skies by Clarence Urmy

California skies!
Balm for the eyes!
Where orange trees or redwoods rise;
By Shasta's snow, Diego's sand,
Or old Diablo's dream set land;

By San Francisco Bay so blue,
Or down some cypress avenue
Near Monterey; by lake, Sierra rimmed,
Or yet afar in valleys vineyard trimmed;
On plain where Ceres waves her wand,
Or where Pomona fond
And all her train in foothill orchards drowse
Under low bending boughs—
Look up!
And from the turquoise cup
Drain dreams and rest!
Ah, none so blest
As one who, weary of life's endless quest
In this fair meadow, poppy pillowed, lies,
Day dreaming 'neath these California skies—
Balm for the eyes!

Yosemite by Daniel S. Richardson

In this deep cleft, so set apart—
So close to Nature's throbbing heart—
I stand in fear,
For God is near.

With wondering eyes, from dizzy trails,
I look on floods and granite vales,
And in them see
Divinity.

From towering cliffs and ice-hewn crown
The arrow-feathered pines look down
Where God alone
Has set His throne.

Be still my soul; the Presence greet.
Unclasp the sandals from thy feet,
For all around—
'Tis holy ground.

Junipero Serra by Richard Edward White

Within the ruined church at Carmel's bay,
Beside the altar, with rank weeds o'ergrown,
There's a grave unmarked with slab or stone,
Where lies one who, lost sight of in our day,
Yet bides his time; and when have passed away
Our would-be heroes, he will then be known,

And glory's heritage at last will own,
His title to which no one will gainsay.
When life was nearing to an end, 'twas here,
Seeking repose, the Padre Serra came;
Of our fair land he was the pioneer:
And if the good alone were known to fame,
Within our hearts his memory would be dear,
And on our lips a household word his name.

To the Colorado Desert by Madge Morris Wagner

Thou brown, bare-breasted, voiceless mystery,
Hot sphinx of nature, cactus-crowned, what hast thou done?
Unclothed and mute as when the groans of chaos turned
Thy naked burning bosom to the sun.
The mountain silences have speech, the rivers sing.
Thou answerest never unto anything.
Pink-throated lizards pant in thy slim shade;
The horned toad runs rustling in the heat;
The shadowy gray coyote, born afraid,
Steals to some brackish spring and laps, and prowls
Away, and howls and howls and howls and howls,
Until the solitude is shaken with an added loneliness.
Thy sharp mescal shoots up a giant stalk,
Its century of yearning, to the sunburnt skies,
And drips rare honey from the lips
Of yellow waxen flowers, and dies.
Some lengthwise sun-dried shapes with feet and hands
And thirsty mouths pressed on the sweltering sands,
Mark here and there a gruesome graveless spot
Where some one drank thy scorching hotness, and is not.
God must have made thee in his anger, and forgot.

Music by Edward Robeson Taylor

The murmurous monotone of waving grain
When winds are gently winging down the vale;
The storm-voiced billows drowning men bewail;
The pattering stroke of softly falling rain;
The sighing leaves that bend to every tale
The breezes tell; the songster's lilting strain,
From feeblest note of all the joyful train
To rapturous burst of peerless nightingale;
What are all these, and all that human ear
In sweetest concord from their kin can hear,
But hints of deeper rhythms as yet unheard;
That in the soul ineffable of things

An ordered Music, by the eternal word,
Throughout the vast of space divinely sings.

In men whom men pronounce divine,
I find so much of sin and blot;
In men whom men denounce as ill
I find so much of goodness still,
I hesitate to draw the line
Between the two, when God has not.

Fair are the flowers and the children, but their subtle suggestion is fairer;
Rare is the roseburst of dawn, but the secret that clasps it is rarer;
Sweet the exultance of song, but the strain that precedes it is sweeter;
And never was poem yet writ, but the meaning outmastered the meter.

Never a daisy that grows, but a mystery guideth the growing;
Never a river that flows, but a majesty scepters the flowing;
Never a Shakespeare that soared, but a stronger than he did enfold him,
Nor ever a prophet foretells, but a mightier seer hath foretold him.

Back of the canvas that throbs the painter is hinted and hidden;
Into the statue that breathes the soul of the sculptor is bidden;
Under the joy that is felt lie the infinite issues of feeling;
Crowning the glory revealed is the glory that crowns the revealing.

Great are the symbols of being, but that which is symboled is greater;
Vast the create and beheld, but vaster the inward creator;
Back of the sound broods the silence, back of the gift stands the giving;
Back of the hand that receives thrill the sensitive nerves of receiving.

Space is as nothing to spirit, the deed is outdone by the doing;
The heart of the wooer is warm, but warmer the heart of the wooing;
And up from the pits where these shiver, and up from the heights where those shine,
Twin voices and shadows swim starward, and the essence of life is divine.

Can this be Christmas—sweet as May,
With drowsy sun, and dreamy air,
And new grass pointing out the way
For flowers to follow, everywhere?

Has time grown sleepy at his post,
And let the exiled Summer back,
Or is it her regretful ghost,
Or witchcraft of the almanac?

Before me, on the wide, warm bay,
A million azure ripples run;
Round me the sprouting palm-shoots lay
Their shining lances to the sun.

With glossy leaves that poise or swing,
The callas their white cups unfold,
And faintest chimes of odor ring
From silver bells with tongues of gold.

A languor of deliciousness
Fills all the sea-enchanted clime;
And in the blue heavens meet, and kiss,

Luke by F. Bret Harte

Wot's that you're readin'?—a novel? A novel,—well, dern my skin!
You a man grown and bearded and histin' such stuff ez that in,—
Stuff about gals and their sweethearts! No wonder you're thin ez a knife.
Look at me!—clar two hundred,—and never read one in my life!

That's my opinion o' novels. And ez to their lyin' round here,
They belonged to the Jedge's daughter,—the Jedge who came up last year
On account of his lungs and the mountains and the balsam o' pine and fir;
And his daughter,—well, she read novels, and that's what's the matter with her.

Yet she allers was sweet on the Jedge, and she stuck by him day and night,
Alone in the cabin up yer,—till she grew like a ghost, all white.
She wus only a slip of a thing, ez light and ez up and away
Ez rifle-smoke blown through the woods, but she wasn't my kind,—no way!

Speaking o' gals, d'ye mind that house ez you rise the hill,
A mile and a half from White's, and jist above Mattingly's mill?
You do? Well now thar's a gal! What, you saw her? Oh, come now, thar, quit!
She was only bedevilin' you boys, for to me she don't cotton one bit.

Now she's what I call a gal,—ez pretty and plump ez a quail;
Teeth ez white ez a hound's and they'd go through a tenpenny nail;
Eyes that kin snap like a cap. So she asked to know "whar I was hid."
She did! Oh, it's jist like her sass, for she's peart ez a Katy-did.

But what was I talking of?—Oh, the Jedge and his daughter,—she read
Novels the whole day long, and I reckon she read them abed,

And sometimes she read them out loud to the Jedge on the porch where he sat,
And 't was how "Lord Augustus" said this, and how "Lady Blanche" she said that.

But the sickest of all that I heerd, was a yarn thet they read 'bout a chap,
"Leather-stocking" by name, and a hunter chock full o' the greenest o' sap;
And they asked me to hear, but I says, "Miss Mabel, not any for me;
When I likes I kin sling my own lies, and thet chap and I shouldn't agree."

Yet somehow or other she was always sayin' I brought her to mind
Of folks about whom she had read, or suthin belike of thet kind,
And thar warn't no end o' the names that she give me thet summer up there,
"Robin Hood," "Leather-stocking," "Rob Roy,"—Oh, I tell you, the critter was queer.

And yet ef she hadn't been spiled, she was harmless enough in her way.
She could jabber in French to her dad, and they said that she knew how to play,
And she worked me that shot-pouch up thar,—which the man doesn't live ez kin use,
And slippers—you see 'em down yer—ez would cradle an Injin's pappoose.

Yet along o' them novels, you see she was wastin' and mopin' away,
And then she got shy with her tongue, and at last she had nothin' to say;
And whenever I happened around, her face it was hid by a book,
And it was n't until she left that she give me ez much ez a look.

And this was the way it was. It was night when I kem up here
To say to 'em all "good by," for I reckoned to go for deer
At "sun up" the day they left. So I shook 'em all round by the hand,
'Cept Mabel, and she was sick, ez they give me to understand.

But jist ez I passed the house next morning at dawn, some one,
Like a little waver o' mist, got up on the hill with the sun;
Miss Mabel it was, all alone,—wrapped up in a mantle o' lace,—
And she stood there straight in the road, with a touch o' the sun in her face.

And she looked me right in the eye,—I'd seen suthin like it before
When I hunted a wounded doe to the edge o' the Clear Lake shore,
And I had my knee on its neck, and jist was a raisin' my knife
When it give me a look like that, and—well, it got off with its life.

"We are going to-day," she said, "and I thought I would say good-by
To you in your own house, Luke,—these woods, and the bright blue sky!
You 've always been kind to us, Luke, and papa has found you still
As good as the air he breathes, and wholesome as Laurel Tree Hill.

"And we'll always think of you, Luke, as the thing we could not take away;
The balsam that dwells in the woods, the rainbow that lives in the spray.
And you'll sometimes think of me, Luke, as you know you once used to say,
A rifle-smoke blown through the woods, a moment, but never to stay."

And then we shook hands. She turned, but a-suddent she tottered and fell,
And I caught her sharp by the waist, and held her a minit,—well,
It was only a minit, you know, that ez cold and ez white she lay

Ez a snow-flake here on my breast, and then—well, she melted away—

And was gone ... And thar are her books; but I says not any for me,
Good enough may be for some, but them and I might n 't agree.
They spiled a decent gal ez might hev made some chap a wife,
And look at me!—clar two hundred,—and never read one in my life!

The Comet by Charles Warren Stoddard

Was it a star,
Or was it a pearl,
Loosed with a jar
From its setting
I' the coronet moon,
And begetting,
As it fell with a whirl
Whirling far—
A splendor that faded too soon?

Was it a dream
Of some splendid star born,
That glowed with a gleam
And a quiver
That startled the night?
Like a river
That flowed to the moon
It did seem,
In its luminous, lustrous light.

Was it a gem
Transfixed with a ray
From the burning, bright hem
Of the wondrous,
Terrible sun, or the moon?
Over us, under us,
Nor night, no, nor day
Hath its equal, bright gem,
Fair feather of light, flown too soon.

Belle of Monterey by Einnim Havemeyer Tucker

In the old and timeworn casa
With its white adobe walls,
The court with its wild grown flowers,
And the stone-paved Spanish halls,

She lives—the slim, dark woman

With the pale Madonna face,
And the brown hands ever weaving,
Fold on fold of cobweb lace.

From the town of San Francisco,
To the shores of Carmel Bay,
She was known "Donna Maria"
As the "Belle of Monterey."

The man whose youth had left him,
The boy with fresh, fair face
And the dark browed Hidalgo
Strove to find in her heart his place.

But though her lovers were legion,
There was one apart from the rest,
And of all the gay throng 'round her,
She loved that man the best.

But his home was not in the West-lands
And his heart was with his home,
So Donna Maria in her casa
Lives year after year alone.

And yesterday we found her
With her inborn Spanish grace.
She showed us her flower garden,
And the quaint old foreign place.

She brought out all her treasures,
And from wrappings yellowed by time,
There came that aroma of romance,
Born only by Spain's sunny clime.

The rebosas, the old mantillas,
Fans, jewels, and rare fine lace,
Told more of the past and its memories,
Than that calm, passionless face.

So to the treasured mementoes,
She clings—the last of her race—
And will die where she passed her girlhood
Of her story leaving no trace.

She waved us a last "Adois"
From the casa's open door,
Round which the tall, grim cacti
Stood like sentinels of war.

And her words like vespers linger,
With the spell that about her lay

Sweet, courtly Donna Maria
The once "Belle of Monterey."

"The Pride of Battery B" by Frank H. Gassaway

South Mountain towered on our right,
Far off the river lay,
And over on the wooded height
We held their lines at bay.

At last the mutt'ring guns were stilled,
The day died slow and wan.
At last the gunners' pipes were filled,
The Sergeant's yarns began.

When,—as the wind a moment blew
Aside the fragrant flood
Our brierwoods raised,—within our view
A little maiden stood.

A tiny tot of six or seven,
From fireside fresh she seemed.
Of such a little one in heaven
I know one soldier dreamed.

And, as we stared, her little hand
Went to her curly head
In grave salute. "And who are you?"
At length the Sergeant said.

"And where's your home?" he growled again.
She lisped out, "Who is me?
Why, don't you know? I'm little Jane,
The Pride of Battery 'B.'

My home? why, that was burned away,
And pa and ma are dead,
And so I ride the guns all day
Along with Sergeant Ned,

And I've a drum that's not a toy,
A cap with feathers, too,
And I march beside the drummer boy
On Sundays at review;

But now our bacca's all give out,
The men can't have their smoke,
And so they're cross—why, even Ned
Won't play with me and joke.

And the big Colonel said to-day—
I hate to hear him swear—
He'd give a leg for a good smoke
Like the Yanks had over there.

And so I thought when beat the drum,
And the big guns were still,
I'd creep beneath the tent and come
Out here across the hill,

And beg, good Mister Yankee men,
You'd give me some Lone Jack,
Please do—when we get some again
I'll surely bring it back.

Indeed I will, for Ned—says he—
If I do what I say
I'll be a General yet, may be,
And ride a prancing bay."

We brimmed her tiny apron o'er,
You should have heard her laugh
As each man from his scanty store
Shook out a gen'rous half.

We gave her escort, till good-night
The little waif we bid,
Then watched her toddle out of sight;
Or else 'twas tears that hid

Her baby form, nor turned about
A man, nor spoke a word
Till after while a far, faint shout
Upon the wind we heard!

We sent it back—then cast sad eye
Upon the scene around.
A baby's hand had touched the tie
That brothers once had bound.

That's all—save when the dawn awoke
Again the work of hell.
And through the sullen clouds of smoke
The screaming missiles fell;

Our General often rubbed his glass,
And marveled much to see
Not a single shell that whole day fell
In the lines of Battery "B!"

If I have faltered more or less
In my great task of happiness;
If I have moved among my race
And shown no glorious morning face;
If beams from happy human eyes
Have moved me not; if morning skies,
Books, and my food, and summer rain
Knocked on my sullen heart in vain:—
Lord, Thy most pointed pleasure take
And stab my spirit broad awake;
Or, Lord, if too obdurate I,
Choose Thou, before that spirit die,
A piercing pain, a killing sin,
And to my dead heart run them in!

A thunderstorm of the olden days!
The red sun' sinks in a sleepy haze;
The sultry twilight, close and still,
Muffles the cricket's drowsy trill.
Then a round-topped cloud rolls up the west,
Black to its smouldering, ashy crest,
And the chariot of the storm you hear,
With its jarring axle rumbling near;
Till the blue is hid, and here and there
The sudden, blinding lightnings glare.
Scattering now the big drops fall,
Till the rushing rain in a silver wall
Blurs the line of the bending elms,
Then blots them out and the landscape whelms.
A flash—a clap, and a rumbling peal:
The broken clouds the blue reveal;
The last bright drops fall far away,
And the wind, that had slept for heat all day,
With a long-drawn sigh awakes again
And drinks the cool of the blessed rain.

November! night, and a sleety storm:
Close are the ruddy curtains, warm
And rich in the glow of the roaring grate.
It may howl outside like a baffled fate,
And rage on the roof, and lash the pane
With its fierce and impotent wrath in vain.
Sitting within at our royal ease

We sing to the chime of the ivory keys,
And feast our hearts from script and score
With the wealth of the mellow hearts of yore.

A winter's night on a world of snow!
Not a sound above, not a stir below:
The moon hangs white in the icy air,
And the shadows are motionless everywhere.
Is this the planet that we know—
This silent floor of the ghostly snow?
Or is this the moon, so still and dead,
And yonder orb far overhead,
With its silver map of plain and sea,
Is that the earth where we used to be?
Shall we float away in the frosty blue
To that living, summer world we knew,
With its full, hot heart-beats as of old,
Or be frozen phantoms of the cold?

A river of ice, all blue and glare,
Under a star-shine dim and rare.
The sheeny sheet in the sparkling light
Is ribbed with slender wisps of white—
Crinkles of snow, that the flying steel
Lightly crunches with ringing heel.
Swinging swift as the swallows skim,
You round the shadowy river's rim:
Falling somewhere out of the sky
Hollow and weird is the owlet's cry;
The gloaming woods seem phantom hosts,
And the bushes cower in the snow like ghosts.

Till the tinkling feet that with you glide
Skate closer and closer to your side,
And something steals from a furry muff,
And you clasp it and cannot wonder enough
That a little palm so soft and fair
Could keep so warm in the frosty air.

'T is thus we dream in our tranquil clime,
Rooted still in the olden time;
Longing for all those glooms and gleams
Of passionate Nature's mad extremes.
Or was it only our hearts, that swelled
With the youth and life and love they held?

Invocation to California by Charles Keeler

Guerdon of gold of the sun is thy treasure

From glist'ning Sierra to foam of the ocean,
With fair flower-children in hosts beyond measure
To yield thee their beauty with boundless devotion!

Royal the reaches of wheat in the valley!
Abundance has blessed the wide wastes of the plain,
And hosts of the strong-handed harvesters rally
At dawn-flush to garner the glittering grain.

Full hang thy orchards with fruitage of summer,
Thy citrons 'mid blossoms bless winter and spring,
But autumn, the radiant year-cycle's last comer,
Bears, clustered in purple, the grape which is king.

Gold, in thy rock-girded fastnesses hidden,
The magic of science shall wrest from its store;
Insatiate progress, advancing, has bidden
That bounty of earth be for man evermore:

For man as a trust and a torch, not to squander
In riotous revel through profitless years,
But a power that bids him to pause and to ponder
On being and beauty, on triumph and tears!

Here, here where the breezes of freedom are blowing,
Shall beauty burst into full flow'rage to-day,
And the will to do right shall, in proud hearts, be growing,
With might to command and with strength to obey.

The Black Vulture by George Sterling

Aloof upon the day's immeasured dome,
He holds unshared the silence of the sky.
Far down his bleak, relentless eyes descry
The eagle's empire and the falcon's home—
Far down, the galleons of sunset roam;
His hazards on the sea of morning lie;
Serene, he hears the broken tempest sigh
Where cold sierras gleam like scattered foam.

And least of all he holds the human swarm—
Unwitting now that envious men prepare
To make their dream and its fulfilment one,
When, poised above the caldrons of the storm,
Their hearts, contemptuous of death, shall dare
His roads between the thunder and the sun.

Resurgam by David Lesser Lezinsky

Ye days of April came so sweet
I seemed to hear the flowers' feet
Come running upward 'neath the sod
Yearning to lift their heads to God!
The days of April.

Just California by John S. McGroarty

'Twixt the seas and the deserts,
'Twixt the wastes and the waves,
Between the sands of buried lands
And the ocean's coral caves,
It lies not East nor West,
But like a scroll unfurled,
Where the hand of God hath hung it,
Down the middle of the world.

It lies where God hath spread it,
In the gladness of his eyes,
Like a flame of jeweled tapestry
Beneath His shining skies,
With the green of woven meadows,
And the hills in golden chains,
The light of leaping rivers,
And the flash of poppied plains.

Days rise that gleam in glory,
Days die with sunset's breeze,
While from Cathay that was of old
Sail countless argosies;
Morns break again in splendor
O'er the giant, new-born West,
But of all the lands God fashioned,
'Tis this land is the best.

Sun and dews that kiss it,
Balmy winds that blow,
The stars in clustered diadems
Upon its peaks of snow;
The mighty mountains o'er it,
Below, the white seas swirled—
Just California stretching down
The middle of the world.

The Happiest Heart by John Vance Cheney

Who drives the horses of the sun
Shall lord it but a day;
Better the lowly deed were done,
And kept the humble way.

The rust will find the sword of fame,
The dust will hide the crown;
Ay, none shall nail so high his name
Time will not tear it down.

The happiest heart that ever beat
Was in some quiet breast
That found the common daylight sweet,
And left to Heaven the rest.

The Creed of Desire by Bruce Porter

Still to be sure of the dawn—
Still to be glad for the sea—
Still to know fire of the blood:
God keep these gifts in me!

Then—I shall cleave the dark!
Then, I shall breast the redoubt!
Then I shall glory the Lord—
And go down to the grave with a shout!

To San Francisco by Samuel John Alexander

If we dreamed that we loved Her aforetime, 'twas the ghost of a dream; for I vow
By the splendour of God in the highest, we never have loved Her till now.
When Love bears the trumpet of Honour, oh, highest and clearest he calls,
With the light of the flaming of towers, and the sound of the rending of walls.
When Love wears the purple of Sorrow, and kneels at the altar of Grief,
Of the flowers that spring in his footsteps, the white flower of Service is chief.
As a flower on the snow of Her bosom, as a star in the night of Her hair,
We bring to our Mother such token as the time and elements spare.

If we dreamed that we loved Her aforetime, adoring we kneel to Her now,
When the golden fruit of the ages falls, swept by the wind from the bough.
The beautiful dwelling is shattered, wherein, as a queen at the feast,
In gems of the barbaric tropics and silks of the ultimate East,
Our Mother sat throned and triumphant, with the wise and the great in their day.
They were captains, and princes, and rulers; but She, She was greater than they.

We are sprung from the builders of nations; by the souls of our fathers we swear,

By the depths of the deeps that surround Her, by the height of the heights She may dare,
Though the Twelve league in compact against Her, though the sea gods cry out in their wrath.
Though the earth gods, grown drunk of their fury, fling the hilltops abroad in Her path,
Our Mother of masterful children shall sit on Her throne as of yore,
With Her old robes of purple about Her, and crowned with the crowns that She wore.

She shall sit at the gates of the world, where the nations shall gather and meet,
And the East and the West at Her bidding shall lie in a leash at Her feet.

The Shrine of Song by Louis Alexander Robertson

In mute amazement oft I pause before
The portals of Song's shrine and list to those
Whose music from its classic cloisters flows
Adown the tide of Time for evermore.
I see the place that no man may explore,
Save him whose Art its life to Genius owes,
On whose rapt lips the sacred cinder glows
That teaches Song's sweet shibboleth and lore.

Ah, it were heaven to enter in and kneel
In some dim aisle, unnoticed and apart,
With thirsting soul to drink the sounds that shame
My songs to silence; then to rise and feel
That my untutored lips had learnt the art
That seats the singer in the House of Fame!

The Rosary by Robert Cameron Rogers

The hours I spent with thee, dear heart,
Are as a string of pearls to me:
I count them over every one apart,
My Rosary, my Rosary.

Each hour a pearl, each pearl a prayer,
To still a heart in absence wrung:
I tell each bead unto the end,
And there a cross is hung!

O memories that bless and burn!
O barren gain and bitter loss!
I kiss each bead, and strive at last to learn
To kiss the cross; sweetheart! to kiss the cross.

Lines by Yone Noguchi

I love the saintly chant of the winds touching their odorous fingers to the harp of the angel, spring;
I love the undiscording sound of thousands of birds, whose concord of song echoes on the rivulet afar;
I muse on the solemn mountain which waits in sound content for the time when the Lord calls forth;
I roam with the wings of high-raised fantasy in the pure Universe;
Oh, I chant of the Garden of Adam and Eve!

The Old Brooch by Charles F. Lummis

Written first in Spanish and then Englished

"Ensueno," osito osado,
Dime, ¿que vayas pensando,
Negrito bendito y feliz,
Alli donde estás reposando,
Tu con la Emperatriz?
Dime, (que ya me deliro)—
¿Que está tu Almohada soñando?
¿A tí una lágrima dando—
Y al Oso Mayor un suspiro?

Little jet bear on a bed of snow,
What are you thinking? As I would think
If I were trembling on that dear brink?
Or are you dizzy as I would be there?
What do you wonder? What do you know?
Are you too happy to know or wonder—
Her throat above you, her bosom under?
Tell, me, what is your Pillow dreaming?
Catch you ever a tear to drink?
Ever a sigh or a flutter, seeming
Maybe a Memory stirred for me there?

The Wolves of the Sea by Herbert Bashford

From dusk until dawn they are hurrying on,
Unfetterd and fearless they flee;
From morn until eve they plunder and thieve—
The hungry, white wolves of the Sea!

With never a rest, they race to the west,
To the Orient's rim do they run;
By the berg and the floe of the northland they go
And away to the isles of the sun.

They wail at the moon from the desolate dune
Till the air has grown dank with their breath;
They snarl at the stars from the treacherous bars

Of the coasts that are haunted by Death.

They grapple and bite in a keen, mad delight
As they feed on the bosom of Grief;
And one steals away to a cave with his prey,
And one to the rocks of the reef.

With the froth on their lips they follow the ships,
Each striving to lead in the chase;
Since loosed by the hand of the King of their band
They have known but the rush of the race.

They are shaggy and old, yet as mighty and bold
As when God's freshest gale set them free;
Not a sail is unfurled in a port of the world
But is prey for the wolves of the Sea!

A Dream of Beauty by Clark Ashton Smith

I dreamed that each most lovely, perfect thing
That Nature hath, of sound, and form, and hue—
The winds, the grass, the light-concentering dew,
The gleam and swiftness of the sea-bird's wing;
Blueness of sea and sky, and gold of storm
Transmuted by the sunset, and the flame
Of autumn-colored leaves, before me came,
And, meeting, merged to one diviner form.

Incarnate Beauty 'twas, whose spirit thrills
Through glaucous ocean and the greener hills,
And in the cloud-bewildered peaks is pent.
Like some descended star she hovered o'er,
But as I gazed, in doubt and wonderment,
Mine eyes were dazzled, and I saw no more.

Women's Eyes by Arthur William Ryder

The world is full of women's eyes,
Defiant, filled with shy surprise,
Demure, a little overfree,
Or simply sparkling roguishly;
It seems a gorgeous lily-bed,
Whichever way I turn my head.

The Goblin Laugh by Edwin Markham

When I behold how men and women grind
And grovel for some place of pomp or power,
To shine and circle through a crumbling hour,
Forgetting the large mansions of the mind,
That are the rest and shelter of mankind;
And when I see them come with wearied brains
Pallid and powerless to enjoy their gains,
I seem to hear a goblin laugh unwind.

And then a memory sends upon its billow
Thoughts of a singer wise enough to play,
Who took life as a lightsome holiday:
Oft have I seen him make his arm a pillow,
Drink from his hand, and with a pipe of willow
Blow a wild music down a woodland way.

The Awakening by Christian Binkley

I see the mystery of life anew,
Bright angels have passed by me: I have heard
A whirr of wings, and voices in adieu.
Now all that seems is hushed, scarcely are stirred
The curtains of the soul, and all things seem
Brooding, and big with portents like the night.
But now I thought I saw the distant gleam
Of angel pinions in the western light,
And heard the fading music: then it rolled
In floods of living sound; and as they swept
Around, in whispered awe they spoke and told
The secrets of the universe. I kept
The fragments that I heard: now all things are
Lit with a glory not of sun or star.

A Nosegay by Augustin S. Macdonald

Of mignonette, a soft sweet spray,
Violets smile a sunbeam's ray,
Pansies mingled, for a thought—
Something that cannot be bought.
All delicately as the fragrance,
Exhale his love's heartfelt cadence.

Appearances by William Henry Hudson

In the city of my dreams,
Where at times I dwell apart,
Nothing is, but only seems—
In the city of my dreams.

And I find them lovelier far,
Deep within my secret heart,
Things that seem than things that are—
Yes, I find them lovelier far!

I am glad that in my dreams
Nothing is, but only seems!

The Grave of Pompey by Sister Anthony, S.N.D.

A wave-scarred rock beside a stranger sea,
The rugged sculpture of a fettered hand,
A Name, rude lettering from a smoking brand.
"Magnus!" Sublime its silent mockery.
And this the End! The triumph car, the train
Of weary captives and the clamorous throng
Up the broad streets; the Senate's proud acclaim;
The storied Column, writ with woe and wrong;
The breathing marble, and the drooping bay,
And the last heart-throes of the Nation's pain,
This, this the End! Come ye who look to Fame
Come, Pride of Power, and gaze on Destiny,
Only the drifting of the desert sand,
Only the moan of the eternal Sea.

Vivérols by David Starr Jordan

Beyond the sea, I know not where,
There is a town called Vivérols;
I know not if 'tis near or far,
I know not what its features are,
I only know 'tis Vivérols.

I know not if its ancient walls
By vine and moss be overgrown;
I know not if the night-owl calls
From feudal battlements of stone
Inhabited by him alone;

I know not if mid meadow-lands
Knee-deep in corn stands Vivérols;
I know not if prosperity

Has robbed its life of poësy.
It could not be in Vivérols,
They would not call it Vivérols.

Perchance upon its terraced heights
The grapes grow purple in the sun;
Or down its wild untrodden crags,
Its broken cliffs and frost-bit jags,
The mountain brooks unfettered run.

I cannot fancy Vivérols
A place of gaudy pomp and show,
A "Grand Establishment des Eaux,"
Where to win back their withered lives
The roués of the city go.

Nor yet a place where poverty
No ray of happiness lets in;
Where wanders hopeless beggary
Mid scenes of sorrow, want and sin,
It cannot be in Vivérols,
There's life and cheer in Vivérols!

Perhaps among the clouds it lies
Mid vapors out from Dreamland blown;
Built up from vague remembrances
That never yet had form in stone
Its castles built of cloud alone.

I only know, should you and I
Through its old walls of crumbling stone
With moss and ivy overgrown
Together wander all alone,

No spot on Earth could be more fair
Than ivy-covered Vivérols;
No grass be greener anywhere
No bluer sky, nor softer air
Than we should find in Vivérols,
Together find in Vivérols.

Love, we may wander far or near,
The sun shines o'er Vivérols,
Green is the grass, the skies are clear:
No clouds obscure our pathway, dear,
Where Love is there is Vivérols,
There is no other Vivérols.

A Memory by Carolus Ager (Charles Kellogg Field)

October fulness in field and flowers,
The ebbing tide of the summer time
In mellow music of days and hours
That beat in rhythm and blend in rhyme;
Leaves that tremble before their turning,
The green that fades and the gold that grows,
A stifled brook, and a throb of yearning
In all that changes for all that goes!

A Toast by Gelett Burgess

Here's to the cause, let who will get the glory!
Here's to the cause, and a fig for the story!
The braggarts may tell it, who serve but for fame;
There'll be more than enough that will die for the name!
And though, in some eddy, our vessels, unsteady,
Be stranded and wrecked, ere the victory's won,
Let the current sweep by us! O death! Come and try us!
What if laggards win praise, if the cause shall go on?

To the Average Man by Wallace Irwin

The average man wears the average clothes
And the average hat on his head;
He eats at a table and sits on a chair
And (normally) sleeps on a bed;
For he scorns the eccentric, and never would dare
To sleep on a table or eat on a chair.

The Average Man seeks the corner saloon
Omeric refreshment to find;
But, shunning the tipple, he wanders to church
Where he is devoutly inclined—
Nor does he expect to find whiskey or dice
In the place that is famed for religious advice.

The Average Man says the average things
And sings just the average songs;
He's deucedly fond of the Average Girl,
For whom he unceasingly longs—
And his vices and virtues, too many to tell,
Are oddly at odds—but they average well.

Statistics declare that the Average Man
Finds the Average Woman and mates;
That the Average Family, children all told,

Is something like two and three-eighths.
(Though fractional children disturb and appal,
The Average Man isn't worried at all.)

The Average Man reads the average books,
And sometimes he writes 'em, I hear;
He's neither a genius, a knave, nor a fool,
In fact he despises the queer;
For if he departed the Average Plan
He'd cease to be known as the Average Man.

But deep in the breast of the Average Man
The passions of ages are swirled,
And the loves and the hates of the Average Man
Are old as the heart of the world—
For the thought of the Race, as we live and we die,
Is in keeping the Man and the Average high.

Twilight Town by Ralph Erwin Gibbs

Oh, Twilight Town is the other side
Of the Hills of the Sunset Light!
Just on the shore of the Sleepy Tide,
Where the weird dream-ships at anchor ride,
Till they sail away at night.

They sail away over the slumber sea,
And the pilot? None can tell.
But who may the crew and the passengers be?
There's Tommy and Elsie, and several wee
Little scamps that we know well.

With the whitest of carpets the decks are spread
And guarded with golden rails;
Old Santa Claus is the figurehead,—
And soft by a lullaby air they're sped
That billows the misty sails.

Growth of the Soul by James Henry MacLafferty

Climb from the depths of the valley's chill,
Out of the shadows that lurk below,
Nurse at the breast of the throbbing hill,
Grow in thy day as the tall trees grow.
This, Soul of Mine, be thy constant cry;
This, O my Soul, is to never die.

Whence camest thou?—Give it little thought!
Whither?—Ah, let this concern thee more!
Into this state thou art blindly brought;
Out of it see but an open door.
Once past the portal, perhaps 't will be
Growth of today will have made thee free

To My Ink-Well by Lionel Josaphare

Thou blotty bottle, bottle stained and grim,
Thou imp, thou gnome, a moody friend art thou.
And yet thyself I would not trade, I vow,
For golden ink-decanter with a rim
Of pearls and decorations wreathed and slim.
Now tell me, ugly boy with inky brow,
Of some unwritten thoughts, which you allow
To dream awhile within your tranquil brim.
How many black imaginings are there
Waiting to crawl out for my livelihood?
Phantasmas, whims, a poet's morbid ware,
Capricious thoughts, perhaps misunderstood?
All liquid yet and blended in their well;
Some will be born; how many, who can tell?

To a Star-Flower by Edward Howard Griggs

Dear little star-flower abloom at my feet,
What are you waiting for, what is it, Sweet?
Is the ceaseless glare of the sun a pain?
Do you long for a sip of the cool, moist rain?

There are star-flowers, Dear, in the human world,
Children with angel wings half furled,
Who find like you that the sun shines strong,
Who at times like you for the soft rain long.

There are children, Sweet, of an older age,
Who have watched life's miracles stage by stage,
To whom the day seems blank and bare,
And the night and the rain-drops sweet and fair.

For the road of pain outstretches long,
The end must come to the sweetest song,
And the only check to the tears we weep
Is the thought that night will come—and sleep!

Little Memories by Nora May French

My thoughts of you ... although I strain and sigh
At stubborn roots, at boughs that tear my face,
No plants in all my garden grow so high,
Nor fill with sturdier life a wider place.

It pleases me, and wakes an old delight,
To go with wordy shears in idle times
And trim them as a patient gardener might,
Clipping the thorny boughs to curves and rhymes.

If these were all, opposing strength with strength
To make my hurt an easier thing to bear;
If these alone usurped my garden's length,
It would not be so hard—I should not care.

But close against the ground, oh, small and weak!
The trodden flowers, the little memories, grow.
Uprooting fingers press them to my cheek....
Dear heart, I love you, and I miss you so.

The Difference by Augustin S. Macdonald

Commerce, born of selfish struggle,
Once met Worship as a saint,
With his bluff he sought to juggle,
God's truth won without restraint.

Lyric by Howard V. Sutherland

O sweet my loved one, hear my prayer,
Be thou mine own and love me!
So dear art thou, so proud, so fair—
Alas, so far above me.
Yet thou, perchance, dear heart, wilt deign
To soothe a heart long steeped in pain,
For pity is a maiden's gain—
O sweet my loved one, hear!

So oft I've prayed, my heart is sore.
When far from thee I sorrow,
And yet, alas, it pains me more
To meet thee on the morrow.
Ah, would that I were fondly pressed
Against thy true, all sacred breast,

Then, then, ah then, might I find rest—
O sweet my loved one, hear!

Nirvana by Bernard Westermann

There is Amida, sublime and high,
Who far in a Daimyo's garden stands,
Eyes half closed, he has crossed his hands;
He waits for nothing, he cannot die.

He has tasted and drunk of the wines of life,
Of every passion and conquered each,
Till a silent power has changed the strife
To the sentient calm that the soul may reach.

Retrospection by James Rawlins

From the hilltops at sunset, Golden Gate.

Deep in the pitying bosom of the sea,
Ebbs fast the glory of a dying day.
And on the giant battlements
That guard these glowing portals of the night,
Another niche appears, full chiseled, deep.
How many fateful names enregistered
In burning letters on that scroll of Time.

But what of it—What matters that
The chastened page be rudely blotted out
By hands that ever faltered as they wrote;
That ere the cruel ink was scarcely dry,
Hot tears erased the shameful entry?

Nay the thing has passed
And deep within the glowing embers lies
The substance—and the form
Ethereal shapes assume that seem, withal,
On golden pinions to have taken flight
And vanished with the spirits of the night.

Titans of Earth by Harold Symmes

Sierran Summits

Peak upon peak uptowering, these mountain giants rise,

Piercing with their summits the far cerulean skies,—
Mighty shouldered Titans relentlessly uphurled
In the grinding pack and pressure that, battling, builds the world.
With slow corroding fingers Time wears their bastions low,
Wreathing the gaping gashes with garlands of her snow.

Quatrain by Stanley Coghill

A burst of song melodious and wild;
A rush of angels through the waiting air;
A flash of light breaking the growing dark;
And then a death like calm, and then Thy face.

Sonnet by Henriette de Saussure Blanding

Because your thoughts have made my flowers more fair,
My sun more golden and my heaven more blue,
Have made me feel that Nature still is true
Beneath the hostile frown she oft doth wear;
Because your song has taught my lips to sing
With gladness, that were dumb; because your heart
Divined the secret of life's highest Art—
Beauty is touch of cloud in everything—
Because your faith has raised me from the cares
Of blackest Doubt to Hope's all radiant beams,
Revealed the truth of all my fading dreams,
Inspired my loves and purified my prayers;
Because your trust in man's divinity
Has saved my soul, I give my all to thee.

When the Baby Died by A. J. Waterhouse

When the baby died, so fair was she—
Like a lily an angel had dropped for me—
That I said to myself: "She is only asleep,"
And I wondered that others would over her weep:
And I stooped and kissed her, half dreaming she
Would open her blue eyes unto me,
And laugh again as on yesterday,
And dimple and croon in the dear old way—
When the baby died.

When the baby died I could not weep,
And I said: "She is only asleep—asleep
She will wake ere long and I shall hear

The prattle I love beat on my ear."
And I smoothed all gently the golden hair,
And I would not believe she was otherwhere
As I cried, "My darling, look up and see!"
But only the night wind answered me—
When the baby died.

When the baby died—sometimes I start
From a dream at night with a longing heart,
For I fancy I hear through the silence wide
A prattle of words from the babe that died.
Then my hands fell down, though empty they be,
For I know that my darling has gone from me,
And the night creeps into a somber day,
While my heart cries out: "Come back, I pray"—
Since the baby died.

A Wingless One by Herman Scheffauer

When I saw in the vaults of azure and sun,
Like blooms from their fields astray,
On painted wings that fluttered and spun
Two golden butterflies play—
Two flames by an airy love made one
In the heart of the day—

Then I longed for a mate and the gift of wings,
But was doomed on the earth to lie,
Till I cursed the clasp of the marl that clings
To thwart my lust for the sky,
And the mournful hunger of wingless things
For the visions that die.

Wireless by Henry Anderson Lafler

The high stars glimmer in thine iron net,
And winds go whimpering along its wires;
Vast on the dark thy Titan bulk aspires—
A watcher on a lonely parapet!
And far, from hidden isles in ocean set,
Invisibly, yet thrall to thy desires,
They come, on wings nor storm nor darkness tires—
Words that the far-off hearts of men beget.

Gaunt harvester of desperate gulfs of night,
Strange winnower in wide dim vales of air,
Wilt thou yet garner by thy mystic might

Some word to still our ancient long despair?—
A whisper from the infinite?—a breath
Caught from the far unfathomed gulf of death?

The California Eschscholtzia by Amelia Woodward Truesdell

The orange hue of the rainbow
Is not so deep as thine;
More rich than a golden goblet
Influshing with sun-lit wine.

On its calyx of pink thy corolla
Catches sheen from the passing sun,
As if powder of pearls were dusted
And gleamed thy soft gold upon.

Of a truth, the dainty fay-maidens
Must have crimped thine edge so thin
Alike to some fairyland pattern,
On thy stamen for golden pin.

Deep down in the cup of thy petals
One spot of a purple stain,
Where the elves forgot in their revels
The last bright drop to drain.

As the scintillant dust of amber
In the sun does thy pollen shine;
Such powder Queen Mab might covet
To burnish her locks divine.

At dusk thou modestly closest
Thy petals with jealous fold;
All night thou cosily sleepest
In a tent of the cloth of gold.

California Sunrise by W. D. Crabb

A California sunrise, over-fair!
See, scarlet-colored margins fringed with green!
Lo! fields of red and crimson bordered there!
Here, blue expanses spanned with whitened sheen!
Lo! yellow banners floating in the air!
Now, purple pastures sweet as eye hath seen!
Here, pink as blossoms mellow with delight!
O many hued, sky-ocean's painted Bight,
Bent like Benin against the shore of night!

Out in California by C. Brown

Out there in California where the orange turns to gold,
And nature has forgot the art of growing cold,
There is not a day throughout the year the flowers do not grow;
There is not an hour the waters do not unfettered flow,
There is not a single moment that the songsters cease to sing,
And life's a sort of constant race twixt Summer and the Spring.
Why, just to know the joy of it one might his best years give,
Out there in California where it's comfort just to live.

A Flower of the First by Charles S. Aiken

What is that? It's only a rosebud;
'Twas caught as I marched from camp,
As red as the red of her heart's blood—
Tears made its petals so damp.

Who threw it? I can guess the maiden;
What matters her name to you?
For with love that flower is laden;
It says: "Eyes of blue—be true!"

Did she speak? Not a word, just tossed it.
I'd seen her the night before—
It fell, and she thought I'd lost it;
And cried, for she had no more.

To press it? Never mind—don't chaff me;
Love weighs some flowers with dew;
Ah, sweet, red blossom, with tears we
Whisper: "Eyes of brown—be true!"

A Year from Now by Sarah Keppel Vickery

Will I have other thoughts
A year from now?
Will this dear joy still wear its blossomed crown?
And this still dearer sorrow,
Will it then, as now
Lay hands of blest remembrance
On my head?
I gaze into the dimness—
Does there grow, beyond my seeing,

The fair light of stars?
I know not—but Thou knowest—
Thou, to whom tomorrow is to-day—
I rest in Thee.
Deal gently with my years.

When I Am Gone by Isabel Pixley

When I am gone and the grass grows green
O'er the couch where I'm laid to rest,
Will you seek that spot, with a kindly thought
For the one that loved you best?

If you do, and you shed but a single tear,
Though I cannot stretch forth my hand,
A violet blue shall smile up at you
To tell you I understand.

My Retreat by Albert J. Atkins

There is a garden in my heart,
A place from all the world apart,
Where I alone in sorrow move,
Awaiting her whose name is Love;
Here in my hour of deepest night
I turn to find her beacon light.

Sometimes I feel an inner gleam
Of Love's true light, a steadfast beam;
Then comes to me a low, sweet voice,
Which makes my longing soul rejoice;
A message brings of strength, of might,
That gives me courage for the fight.

When weary with the outward strife,
I seek this sacred inner life,
And find within its calm repose,
A brief surcease from earthly woes;
Thus, in the garden of my heart,
I rest from all the world apart.

Whom Does She Love? by Arthur William Ryder

With one she gossips full of art;
Her glances with a second flirt;

She holds another in her heart:
Whom does she love enough to hurt?

Sisters of the Little Sorrows by Juliet Wilbor Tompkins

From visions of gray to-morrows,
All patient and sore dismayed,
Come ye of the Little Sorrows,
To whom no tears are paid:
The hurt, who may not stagger,
Who dare not nurse their stings—
For wounds are of sword and dagger,
And thorns are little things!

'Tis only your beauty failing,
The youth of your heart grown numb?
Ah, sisters, we sit bewailing
Your daily martyrdom:
And she who treads the city
With feet that mourn the wild,
She shares our aching pity;
And she who bears no child;

And she of the crumbling altars;
And she who must earn her bread
By paths where the spirit falters;
And she whose friend is dead;
And she who'd fain recover
The spendthrift days that were;
And the heart that found no lover—
Kind Lord, they laugh at her!

The wounds that are not of sabres
Shall never be understood,
But pity may ease your labors,
O patient Sisterhood!
For there be hearts no sadder,
Nor truer right to mourn,
Though the wasp is not the adder,
One dies not of the thorn.

Daffodils by Grace Hibbard

"If I had but two loaves of bread, I would sell one and buy hyacinths."—The Koran.

O daffodils, bright daffodils,
I'd sell my other loaf for thee.

Thou art so sweet, I love thee so,
That thou art soul-bread unto me.

I've placed thee in a crystal vase,
As clear as crystal vase can be;
Hold high thy pretty yellow heads,
While I a story tell to thee.

Once up each side a garden path
Two lines of daffodils did stray,
Two golden chains of memory,
That link my childhood with to-day.

Up to an old colonial house,
From gate to doorsill, side by side,
Were daffodils in yellow gowns,
Gay daffodils—New England's pride.

A little girl stood in the door,
Her heart was filled with love for thee,
First garden flowers of the spring,
O daffodils, that girl was me.

Confusion by E. F. Green

Pretty Jennie came to me,
Anxious, seeking information.
"Show me, Richard, will you please,
What is meant by osculation?"

What could mortal man as I
Do in such a situation,
Father, Mother, no one by;
Liberal views, a strong temptation?

Jennie is my cousin, too.
So, to please my young relation—
"Oh, you horrid thing, there now,
I referred to occultation."

An Indian Verse by Hu Maxwell

Translated from Language California Indians

Darling mine, sweet mine, we sever.
I am going far from thee.
Must this parting be forever?

Shall we stroll beside the sea
Any more? The sea breeze blowing
Soft I feel upon my brow;
And I see the lightning glowing
On the distant mountain now;
And the verdant valleys under
All the hills are gleaming bright,
Lit by lightning, while the thunder,
Dull and mournful, blends with night.
And, alas! thou art not near me,
And my soul is sad and lone!
Fare thee well. Thou canst not hear me—
All my joy and bliss are flown.

The Stream of Life by Lilian Lauferty

Unknowingly, unceasingly, still day by day they pass us by—
Those friends whom we shall never know—comrades to whom our spirits cry.
A little child may shyly smile, a gray haired man may kindly glance;
But smiling still, they pass the while, and life bears on its puppet dance.

Perhaps that girl with eyes sea gray might be a comrade soul to me;
That lad of spirit blithe and gay may hold to friendship's shrine the key.
But still the stream of life flows by—flows by to some unchartered sea;
A comrade spirit greets the eye, then sweeps away eternally.

With laggard step or joyful feet, at every turn throughout the day
We pass, but we may never meet, for still convention holds her sway.
Brothers and sisters all, they claim—perhaps, but 'tis a weary while.
Since man has dared, unknowing shame, to greet his fellows with a smile.

The Change by Charles Philip Nettleton

Unconsciously we wail with life's first breath,
So dark and dure the past throws down its shade;
But ripening years to strength and peace persuade
Our souls, and consciously, we smile at death.

The Spirit of California by Rufus Steele

I am Ariel freed of a master;
I am Puck lacking Oberon's ban;
When the lotus is ripe, hark my Pandean pipe
For I'm Peter the godchild of Pan.
I am Iris, my brush is a rainbow;

Endymion awakened am I;
In the breast of the tree Hamadryad I be—
With Sequoia I tickle the sky!

In the orchard I hang my round beacons—
Ah, Calypso, less potent thy lute!
And men come to seize and lean strip my trees,
For I'm nectar that sweetens the fruit.
My breath have I blown on the melon:
When the honey bee, laden, starts home
I follow his tracks, leave my kiss on his wax:
The poppy I've sprinkled with chrome.

I mask me in gold in the wheat-fields,
And I laugh at the reaper's sure tread—
The sheaves are alined, it is me they would bind:
I am soul of the grain, I am bread.
In autumn men seek me in vineyards;
The purple which lures them is mine—
"The capture is nigh; quick, the press!" is their cry:
I am blood of the grape, I am wine.

O, I'm secret of life-giving rivers;
I am balm that exhales from Health's cave:
Consumed in each kernel, I live on eternal,
I am Master of Life, I'm its Slave.
From the battlements of the Sierra
The Pandean pipe I swing free,
And my far-floating tune, in the stillness of noon,
Weaves a spell from the peaks to the sea.

Song of the Out-of-Doors by Herbert Bashford

Come with me, O you world-weary, to the haunts of thrush and veery,
To the cedar's dim cathedral and the palace of the pine;
Let the soul within you capture something of the wildwood rapture,
Something of the epic passion of that harmony divine!
Down the pathway let us follow through the hemlocks to the hollow,
To the woven, vine-wound thickets in the twilight vague and old,
While the streamlet winding after is a trail of silver laughter,
And the boughs above hint softly of the melodies they hold.
Through the forest, never caring what the way our feet are faring,
We shall hear the wild birds' revel in the labyrinth of Tune,
And on mossy carpets tarry in His temples cool and airy,
Hung with silence and the splendid, amber tapestry of noon.
Leave the hard heart of the city, with its poverty of pity,
Leave the folly and the fashion wearing out the faith of men,
Breathe the breath of life blown over upland meadows white with clover,
And with childhood's clearer vision see the face of God again!

To William Vaughn Moody by Herbert Heron

The Poet of "The Fire Bringer"

Dead! and we gaze, unseeing, on your bier,
Where westward thunders roll;
But though you die, your living song is clear
(Prometheus lights your goal);
And till we too are taken, we can hear
That music from your soul!

"The Greatest of These Is Charity" by Harriet M. Skidmore

Three kindly angels, crowned with light,
Illumine our way through darkest night.
Safe shall they rest in realms above
Who follow Faith, and Hope, and Love.

But Hope must die, her mission done,
Where blissful certainty is won.
And Faith, when "face to face" we see,
Is lost in glad Reality.

One fadeth not, one dieth ne'er,
But, robed in Heavenly radiance fair,
Shall keep through endless years above
Her glorious name—Immortal Love!

Glose upon a Ruba'iy by Porter Garnett

"A Book of Verses underneath the Bough,
A Jug of Wine, a Loaf of Bread—and Thou
Beside me singing in the Wilderness—
Oh, Wilderness were Paradise enow!"

Oft have the footsteps of my Soul been led
By thee, sweet Omar, far from hum of toil
To where the Chenar trees their plumage spread
And tangly vines of wild-grape thickest coil;
Where distant fields, scarce glimpst in noon content,
Are lush with verdure quick upon the plough;
Where trill of Nightingale beneath the Tent
Of heaven sinks away to soft lament;—
There have I sat with Thee and conned ere now

A Book of Verses underneath the Bough.

When from the city's raucous din new-freed
I quaff thy wisdom from the Clearing Cup
Of Rubaiyat, then, even as I read,
I seem with Thee, in Persian groves to sup
On bread of Yezdakhast and Shiraz Wine
That lifts the net of Care from off the brow.
These words, that tongue the Spirit of the Vine,
Break from the Veil, and lo! the Voice is thine:
Then is my wish—would Fate that wish allow!—
A Jug of Wine, a Loaf of Bread—and Thou.

Although I tread the Wilderness of life,
Thy song can waft me to that careless clime,
Where enter in nor memories of strife,
Nor ghosts of woe from out the Gulf of Time.
There, by thy side, great Omar, would I stray,
And drink the Juice that has forgot the Press,
(A Pot, the Potter shaped but Yesterday—
To-morrow will it be but broken Clay?)
With only Thee the toilsome road to bless,
Beside me singing in the Wilderness.

When thou dost scorn the waste and mourn the Rose,
That dies upon the world's too sinful breast,
In thy disdain a wondrous beauty glows,
Unfolding visions of a Life more blest.
Then from thy Naishapur in Khorasan
I seem to wander, though I know not how,
Within the glittering gates of Jennistan,
Supreme Shadukiam I wondering scan:
Though still I walk the Wilderness, I vow—
Oh, Wilderness were Paradise enow!

The Poet by Ina Coolbrith

He walks with God upon the hills!
And sees, each morn, the world arise
New-bathed in light of paradise.
He hears the laughter of her rills,
Her melodies of many voices,
And greets her while his heart rejoices.
She, to his spirit undefiled,
Makes answer as a little child;
Unveiled before his eyes she stands,
And gives her secrets to his hands.

A Life by Edward Howard Griggs

The stregth of gentleness, the might of meekness,
The glory of a courage unafraid,
A constant love, a tenderness for weakness,
Were in her face and in her life displayed.

In the Redwood Canyons by Lillian H. Shuey

Down in the redwood canyons, cool and deep,
The shadows of the forest ever sleep,
The odorous redwoods, wet with fog and dew,
Touch with the hay and mingle with the yew.
Under the firs the red madroña shines,
The graceful tan oaks, fairest of them all,
Lean lovingly unto the sturdy pines,
In whose far tops the whistling blue-birds call.

Here where the forest shadows ever sleep,
The mountain lily lifts its chalice white,
The myriad ferns hang draperies soft and light
Thick on each mossy bank and watered steep,
Where slender deer tread softly in the night,
Down in the redwood canyons dark and deep.

California by Augustin S. Macdonald

An abundance of sunshine,
A tincture of rain,
Rare atmosphere fine,
Make life thrill again.

Night-Sentries by George Sterling

Ever, as sinks the day on sea or land,
Called or uncalled you take your kindred posts.
At helm and lever, wheel and switch you stand,
On the world's wastes and melancholy coasts.
Strength to the patient hand!
To all, alert and faithful in the night,
May there be Light!

Now roars the wrenching train along the dark:
How many watchers guard the barren way,

In signal-towers, at stammering keys, to mark
What word the whispering horizons say!
To all that see and hark,
To all, alert and faithful in the night,
May there be Light!

On ruthless streets, on by-ways sad with sin,
(Half hated by the blinded ones you guard)
Guard well, lest crime unheeded enter in!
The dark is cruel and the vigil hard.
The hours of guilt begin.
To all, alert and faithful in the night,
May there be Light!

Now reels the pulsing hull adown the sea:
Gaze onward, anxious eyes, to mist or star!
Where foams the heaving highway wide and free?
Where wait the reef, the berg, the cape, the bar?
Whatever menace be,
To all, alert and faithful in the night,
May there be Light!

Now the surf-rumble rides the midnight wind,
And grave patrols are at the ocean-edge.
Now soars the rocket where the billows grind,
Discerned too late, on sunken shoal or ledge.
To all that seek and find,
To all, alert and faithful in the night,
May there be Light!

On lonely headlands gleam the lamps that warn,
Star-steady, or a-blink like dragon-eyes.
Govern your rays, or wake the giant horn
Within the fog that welds the sea and skies!
Far distant runs the morn:
To all, alert and faithful in the night,
May there be Light!

Now glow the lesser lamps in rooms of pain,
Where nurse and doctor watch the joyless breath,
Drawn in a sigh, and sighing lost again.
Who waits without the threshhold, Life or Death?
Reckon you loss or gain?
To all, alert and faithful in the night,
May there be Light!

Honor to you that guard our welfare now!
To you that constant in the past have stood!
To you by whom the future shall avow
Unconquerable fortitude and good!
Upon the sleepless brow

Of each, alert and faithful in the night,
May there be Light!

www.ingramcontent.com/pod-product-compliance
Lightning Source LLC
Chambersburg PA
CBHW060052050426
42448CB00011B/2415